ARROZ CON LECHE
Popular Songs and Rhymes from Latin America

Selected and illustrated by Lulu Delacre

English lyrics by Elena Paz
Musical arrangements by Ana-María Rosado

SCHOLASTIC
HARDCOVER

SCHOLASTIC INC. ▲ New York

To Alicia, who accompanied me until the very end;
and Verónica, a bundle of joy when singing the songs.

A LUCAS ● EVANS BOOK

Library of Congress Cataloging-in-Publication Data
Arroz con leche.   Children's songs of Latin America.
Spanish and English words.   Includes unacc. melodies.   Bibliography: p. 32
Summary: A collection of traditional Latin-American songs and rhymes, in Spanish and English, with the music included.
1. Children's songs — Latin America.   2. Folk songs, Spanish — Latin America.   [1. Folk songs, Spanish — Latin America.   2. Songs, Spanish — Latin America.   3. Spanish language materials — Bilingual]   I. Delacre, Lulu, ill.
M1990.A78   1989   88-751962   ISBN 0-590-41887-4

12 11 10 9 8 7 6 5 4 3 2   9/8 0 1 2 3 4/9

Printed in the U.S.A.   36

First Scholastic printing, April 1989

Contents

¡Qué linda manito!

Qué linda manito
que tiene el bebé,
qué linda, qué mona,
qué bonita es.

Pequeños deditos
rayitos de sol,
que gire que gire
como un girasol.

PUERTO RICO

A Pretty Little Hand

How pretty, how little,
This sweet baby's hand.
So soft — Oh! So pretty!
How lovely it is.

Fingers so tiny
Like small rays of sun,
Around and around
Like a twinkling sunflower.

While singing this song, try moving your hands around and around in a circular motion
for baby to imitate.

Allá en la fuente

Allá en la fuente
había un chorrito;
se hacía grandote,
se hacía chiquito;
estaba de mal humor,
pobre chorrito
tenía calor.

MEXICO

The Fountain

There in the fountain
A little streamlet
Would swell so grandly
Then wither sadly.
It could not but shed a tear.
It felt too hot,
The poor little dear.

Aserrín, aserrán

Aserrín, aserrán
los maderos de San Juan.
Los de Juan comen pan,
los de Pedro comen queso,
los de Enrique, alfeñique . . .
¡Ñique, ñique, ñique!

PUERTO RICO

Sawdust Song

Sawdust sings, sawdust songs,
In the woods of Old San Juan.
John eats bread, if you please,
Peter only gets some cheese.
Happy Henry sucks his candy . . .
Almonds spun with sugar candy.

Children love to sway to the singsong rhythm of this popular song. Hold baby by the hands on your lap, swaying back and forth, until *ñique, ñique, ñique,* when you shake or tickle baby gently.

Naranja dulce

Naranja dulce,
limón partido,
dame un abrazo
que yo te pido.

Si fuera falso
mi juramento,
en poco tiempo
se olvidará.

Toca la marcha
mi pecho llora;
adiós, señora,
yo ya me voy.

MEXICO

10

Orange So Sweet

Orange so sweet
A lemon slice, love,
I'm asking you for
A hug tonight, love.

If I forsake you
While I'm away, dear,
Then please forget me
Forevermore.

Strike up the music
Let it play on, dear,
My poor heart's broken
Dear love, farewell.

Parting is such sweet sorrow, the young soldier sings to his true love as he goes off to join the army. In this popular song-game, children hold hands and form a circle. They select a soldier, who stands in the center, and circle him while he chooses a sweetheart. The two hug and part together from the game. This goes on, until there are no children left in the circle.

11

Un elefante se balanceaba

Un elefante se balanceaba
sobre la tela de una araña,
como veía que resistía
fue a llamar a otro elefante.

Dos elefantes se balanceaban
sobre la tela de una araña,
como veían que resistía
fueron a llamar a otro elefante.

Tres elefantes. . . .
Cuatro elefantes. . . .
Etc. . . .

MEXICO

12

The Graceful Elephant

One elephant balanced gracefully
Upon a spider's web,
But when the web bounced him all around
He called in another to help hold it down.

Two elephants balanced gracefully
Upon a spider's web,
But when the web bounced them all around
They called in another to help hold it down.

Three elephants. . . .
Four elephants. . . .
Etc. . . .

13

Arroz con leche

Arroz con leche se quiere casar
con una viudita de la capital,
que sepa coser, que sepa bordar,
que ponga la aguja en el campanar.

Tilín, tilán, sopitas de pan.
Allá viene Juan, comiéndose el pan.

Yo soy la viudita, la hija del rey,
me quiero casar y no encuentro con quién:
contigo sí, contigo no;
contigo, mi vida, me casaré yo.

Rice and Milk

I'm Rice and Milk, I'd like to be wed,
To a good little widow who bakes a fine bread.
Who knows how to sew and knows how to weave,
And in the bell tower her needle does keep.

Ting-a-ling, ting-a-long. Ting-a-ling, ting-a-long.
With her I will marry, with her I belong.

I am the king's daughter, a good widow, too.
I'd like to get married, I know not with whom.
With you sir, it's yes. With you sir, it's no.
With you dear, I'll marry — let's be married soon.

PUERTO RICO

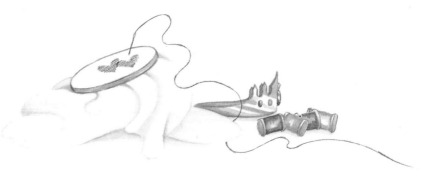

This favorite Latin-American tune is also a game. Here, a widow is chosen to be at the center of the circle. The children hold hands and circle around and around her as she chooses a husband. The widow trades places with the husband, and the game starts anew.

Estaba la pájara pinta

Estaba la pájara pinta
sentada en un verde limón,
con el pico recoge la hoja
con la hoja recoge la flor.
¡Ay, ay, ay! ¿Dónde estará mi amor?

ARGENTINA

The Lovely Bird

Cu-cu-ru! sang the lovely bird,
High up on its lofty crest.
Pecking branches and buds of the lime tree,
She cried as she made her nest:
Oh! Oh! Oh! Where can my true love be?

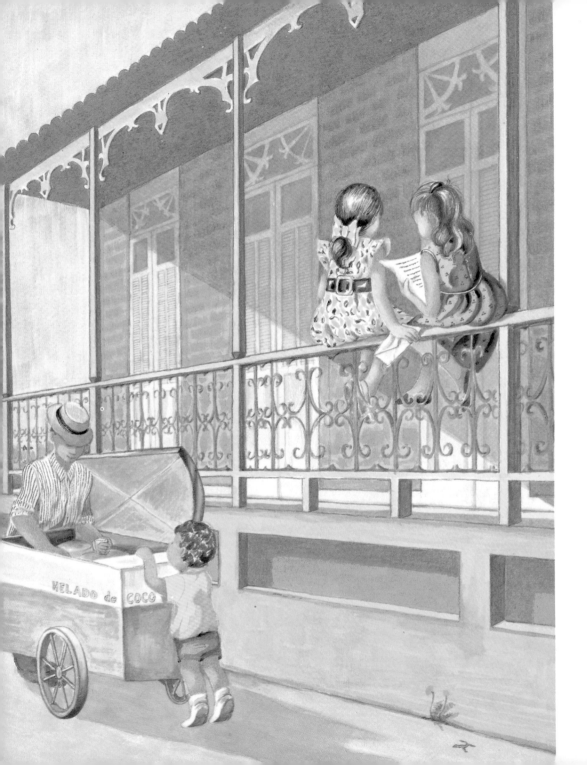

El hijo del conde

El hijo del conde,
      ¡caramba!
me escribió un papel,
que si yo quería,
      ¡caramba!
casarme con él.

Yo le contesté,
      ¡caramba!
en otro papel,
que si me casaba,
      ¡caramba!
no sería con él.

PUERTO RICO

18

The Count's Son

The son of the count,
　　　Oh! Caramba!
Wrote a note to me,
Asking for my hand,
　　　Oh! Caramba!
To be wed to me.

Quickly I replied,
　　　Oh! Caramba!
Here is what I said:
"Should I ever marry,
　　　Caramba!
Not with you!" I said.

19

¡Qué llueva!

¡Qué llueva! ¡Qué llueva!
la virgen de la cueva,
los pajaritos cantan,
las nubes se levantan,

¡Qué sí! ¡Qué no!
¡Qué caiga el chaparrón!

PUERTO RICO

It's Raining!

It's raining! It's raining!
The cavern maiden's calling.
The little birds are singing,
All the clouds are lifting.

Oh yes — Oh no!
Oh! Let the downpour fall.

In Puerto Rico the rain is very special. On a bright, sunny day, there can suddenly be a downpour; and just as suddenly, the rain will stop, and it will be sunny again!

La loba

La loba, la loba,
le compró al lobito,
un calzón de seda
y un gorro muy bonito.

La loba, la loba
se fue de paseo,
con su gorro lindo
y su hijito feo.

ARGENTINA

The She-Wolf

Oh Mama Wolf, Oh Mama Wolf,
For her puppy she did buy
Pretty pantaloons of silk
And a hat so very fine.

Mamita Wolf, Mamita Wolf,
Strolling 'round so grand was she
With her finest bonnet on
And her ugly little son.

Pimpollo de canela

Pimpollo de canela,
flor en capullo,
duérmete, vida mía,
mientras te arrullo.

PUERTO RICO

Cinnamon Shoot

Cinnamon shoot,
Bud in flower,
Sleep my child,
While I cuddle you.

En la puerta del cielo

En la puerta del cielo,
venden zapatos,
para los angelitos
que andan descalzos.

PUERTO RICO

At Heaven's Gate

At heaven's gate
A cobbler so kind
Fits out barefoot angels
With shoes so fine.

¡Qué linda manito!

A Pretty Little Hand

How pretty, how little,
This sweet baby's hand.
So soft — Oh! So pretty!
How lovely it is.

Fingers so tiny
Like small rays of sun,
Around and around
Like a twinkling sunflower.

Qué lin - da ma - ni - to que tie - ne_el be - bé, qué
Pe - que - ños de - di - tos ra - yi - tos de sol, que

lin - da, qué mo - na, qué bo - ni - ta es.
gi - re que gi - re co - mo_un gi - ra - sol.

Allá en la fuente

The Fountain

There in the fountain
A little streamlet
Would swell so grandly
Then wither sadly.
It could not but shed a tear.
It felt too hot,
The poor little dear.

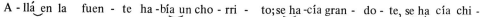

A - llá_en la fuen - te ha -bía un cho - rri - to; se ha -cía gran - do - te, se ha cía chi -

qui - to; es - ta - ba de mal hu - mor, po - bre cho - rri - to te - nía ca - lor.

Aserrín, aserrán

Sawdust Song

Sawdust sings, sawdust songs,
In the woods of Old San Juan.
John eats bread, if you please,
Peter only gets some cheese.
Happy Henry sucks his candy . . .
Almonds spun with sugar candy.

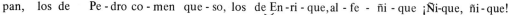

A - se - rrín, a - se - rrán los ma - de - ros de San Juan. Los de Juan co - men

pan, los de Pe - dro co - men que - so, los de_En - ri - que, al - fe - ñi - que ¡Ñi - que, ñi - que!

Naranja dulce

Na -ran -ja dul - ce, li -món par -ti - do, da -me un a - bra - zo que yo te

pi - do. Si fue - ra fal -so mi ju -ra - men -to, en po -co tiem -po se_ol -vi -da-

rá. To -ca la mar -cha mi pe -cho llo - ra; a -diós, se - ño - ra, yo ya me voy.

Orange So Sweet

Orange so sweet
A lemon slice, love,
I'm asking you for
A hug tonight, love.

If I forsake you
While I'm away, dear,
Then please forget me
Forevermore.

Strike up the music
Let it play on, dear,
My poor heart's broken
Dear love, farewell.

Arroz con leche

A - rroz_con le -che se quie -re ca -sar con u -na viu -di -ta de la ca -pi -tal, que
Yo soy la viu -di -ta, la hi -ja del rey, me quie -ro ca -sar y no en -cuen -tro con quién: con-

se -pa co -ser, que se -pa bor -dar, que pon -ga l'a -gu -ja en el cam -pa -nar. Ti-
ti -go sí, con -ti -go no; con -ti -go, mi vi -da, me ca -sa -ré yo. Ti-

lín, ti -lán, so - pi -tas de pan. A - llá vie -ne Juan, co - mién -do -s'el pan.

Rice and Milk

I'm Rice and Milk,
  I'd like to be wed,
To a good little widow
  who bakes a fine bread.
Who knows how to sew
  and knows how to weave,
And in the bell tower
  her needle does keep.

Ting-a-ling, ting-a-long.
  Ting-a-ling, ting-a-long.
With her I will marry,
  with her I belong.

I am the king's daughter,
  a good widow, too.
I'd like to get married,
  I know not with whom.
With you sir, it's yes.
With you sir, it's no.
With you dear, I'll marry —
  let's be married soon.

29

Estaba la pájara pinta

The Lovely Bird

Cu-cu-ru! sang the lovely bird,
High up on its lofty crest.
Pecking branches and buds
   of the lime tree,
She cried as she made her nest:
Oh! Oh! Oh!
   Where can my true love be?

Es - ta - ba la pá - ja - ra pin - ta sen - ta - da en un ver - de li -
món, con el pi - co re - co - ge la ho - ja con la ho - ja re - co - ge la
flor. ¡Ay, ay, ay! ¿Dón - de es - ta - rá mi a - mor?

El hijo del conde

The Count's Son

The son of the count,
     Oh! Caramba!
Wrote a note to me,
Asking for my hand,
     Oh! Caramba!
To be wed to me.

Quickly I replied,
     Oh! Caramba!
Here is what I said:
"Should I ever marry,
     Caramba!
Not with you!" I said.

El hi - jo del con - de, ¡ca - ram - ba! me es-cri-bió un pa - pel, que si yo que -
rí - a, ¡ca - ram - ba! ca - sar - me con él. Yo le con - tes - té, __ ¡ca - ram - ba!
en o - tro pa - pel, que si me ca - sa - ba, ¡ca - ram - ba! no se - ría con él.

¡Qué llueva!

¡Qué llue - va! ¡Qué llue - va! la vir - gen de la cue - va, los

pá - ja - ri - tos can - tan, las nu - bes se le - van - tan, ¡Qué

sí! ¡Qué no! ¡Qué cai - ga el cha - pa - rrón!

It's Raining!

It's raining! It's raining!
The cavern maiden's calling.
The little birds are singing,
All the clouds are lifting.

Oh yes — Oh no!
Oh! Let the downpour fall.

La loba

La lo - ba, la lo - ba, le com - pró al lo - bi - to, un cal - zón de

se - da y un go - rro muy bo - ni - to. La lo - ba, la lo - ba

se fue de pa - se - o, con su go - rro lin - do y su hi - ji - to fe - o.

The She-Wolf

Oh Mama Wolf, Oh Mama Wolf,
For her puppy she did buy
Pretty pantaloons of silk
And a hat so very fine.

Mamita Wolf, Mamita Wolf,
Strolling 'round so grand was she
With her finest bonnet on
And her ugly little son.

Artist's Note

Latin-American folklore is rich in children's songs, games, and rhymes. Many were inherited from Spain and with time, permeated with the local flavor of each country. That is why we find children from different Hispanic countries all singing and dancing to their own local versions of songs like "Arroz con leche." (Each song in this collection is marked either Mexico, Puerto Rico, or Argentina to indicate which country's version was selected.)

Many of the places portrayed here are actual ones, like the view of the Old San Juan Cathedral in Puerto Rico in "Arroz con leche." There are typical things like the balloon seller in "Allá en la fuente," so often seen in and around Mexico City; or the coconut ice cream seller in "El hijo del conde," often found in Puerto Rico. The Indian women in the open market in "Naranja dulce" are dressed in *huipiles* — their typical and beautiful garments for all occasions. And children will love finding the tiny lizards that appear in some of the pictures.

Here is a glimpse of the kaleidoscope of cheerful songs and rhymes from the oral tradition, to be enjoyed by those who know them, and shared to acquaint those who don't with their warmth and charm.

After reading and singing the songs, should you still want an extra-sweet something, go to the kitchen and try the recipe appearing in the book for, of course, *arroz con leche* — rice and milk.

Bibliografía / Bibliography

A la sombra de un verde limón: Antología del cancionero tradicional infantil argentino, Paulina Mousichoff. Biblioteca de Cultura Popular, Ediciones del Sol, 1984.

Cancionero tradicional argentino, Horacio Jorge Becco. Hachette, Buenos Aires, 1960.

El cantar folklórico de Puerto Rico, Marcelino Canino Salgado. Editorial Universitaria, P.R. 1974.

Muestras del folklore puertorriqueño, Marigloria Palma. Editorial Edil, 1981.

Naranja dulce, limón partido, Antología de la lírica infantil mexicana, Mercedes Díaz Roig y María Teresa Miaja; El Colegio de México, 1979.